ABHISHEK KUMAR

PRABHAT
PRAKASHAN

Published by
PRABHAT PRAKASHAN PVT. LTD.
4/19 Asaf Ali Road,
New Delhi-110 002 (INDIA)
e-mail: prabhatbooks@gmail.com

ISBN 978-93-5488-661-4
OPRAH WINFREY: A COMPLETE BIOGRAPHY
by Abhishek Kumar

Edition
First, 2023

Price
₹ 250 (Rupees Two Hundred Fifty Only)

Printed at
Japan Art, Delhi

Author's Note

A google search of Oprah's name opens up a whole Pandora box of websites, blogs and video blogs, dedicated to the Queen of talk shows. But none of them manage to capture completely the phenomena called Oprah Winfrey. In order to understand properly what actually constitutes Oprah, one needs to have a multifaceted perspective towards it. Oprah, unlike any other celebrity, has more facets to her character than one can grasp in a single go. Her influence on culture and society is a subject worth dedicating time to. Her ability to form public opinion through her show and her acts is an unmatched one. Many a times she has been described as one of the most influential personalities on earth. Her endorsement, be it of any book through her book club or of any political personality like Obama, works magically to gain instant recognition and acceptance among the crowd. She embodies the famous phrase, 'with great power comes great responsibilities'. She, as a celebrity, completely realizes her potential to bring change in the lives of many, and she lives up to her potential.

With the help of her private charity, Winfrey has awarded hundreds of grants that support the education of women in the United States and around the world. Through her acts of philanthropy, she has managed to bring remarkable change in the lives of those in need across the globe.

No one word can capture the role that Oprah has played and continues to play in her public life. One might need a multitude of such words in order to cover different aspects of her career. She is an actor, a TV show host, a producer, a writer, a book critic, a philanthropist and also an activist. She is also known to wield a phenomenon called the Oprah effect. Her endorsements multiply exponentially in popularity within weeks of being endorsed. But this only makes her more critical of what she chooses to endorse.

Her influence on her audience goes beyond forming their opinions. She is also a source of inspiration for many. By many she has been called a 'prophet', an 'inspirational phenomenon' and 'almost a religion'. But Oprah chooses to downplay all such claims. She instead never allows her immense success to go beyond her head ever. But this does not mean that her life has been free from controversies. In fact, there is a multitude of those.

Unlike many other talk shows, Oprah made sure that hers remains socially relevant and a medium for a positive change in the society. Throughout her career, she has informed many and opened eyes of the world to the issues people often turn blind eye to.

As an author, researching and writing about Oprah proved to be a true delight. Her life's story carries plenty of inspiration and life lessons. It is my sincere effort that in pages which unfold henceforth, I honestly unfold before the readers the pages of Oprah's life.

❑

Contents

Introduction

Through media, Oprah Winfrey has established an unparalleled connect with the people around the world. She as a host, and supervising producer of the award-winning The Oprah Winfrey Show, has entertained, enlightened and uplifted millions of viewers worldwide for more than 25 years. Her endeavours as a global media trailblazer and philanthropist have proven her as one of the most esteemed and respected public figures today.

Oprah Gail Winfrey was born to Vernita Lee and Vernon Winfrey on a remote farm in Kosciusko, Mississippi, on 29 January 1954. Her name was decided to be Orpah, from the Bible, but because of the trouble of spelling and articulation,

The Oprah Winfrey Show, has entertained, enlightened and uplifted millions of viewers worldwide for more than 25 years.

she was known as Oprah practically since her birth. Her bachelor parents parted soon after she was born and left her in the upkeep of her maternal grandmother on the farm.

As a child, Oprah Winfrey wore potato sacks because clothing did not always fit into the budget of her poverty-stricken family. Today, Forbes estimates Winfrey's net worth at $3 billion, and she is the only black woman on the publication's list of the 400 richest people in America.

During her childhood, she entertained herself by 'playacting' in front of an 'audience' of farm animals. Underneath the strict supervision of her grandmother, she learned to read at two and a half years old. She lectured her church audience about 'when Jesus rose on Easter Day' when she was two years old. Then she hopped kindergarten after lettering a note to her teacher on the first day of school saying she fitted in the first grade. Oprah was upheld to third grade after that year.

Before she became a media mogul and the queen of daytime TV, Winfrey suffered a tumultuous childhood. She was shuffled between family members, spending her first few years on her grandmother's farm in rural Mississippi while her unwed teenage mom looked for work, according to the Academy of Achievement.

As a child, Oprah Winfrey wore potato sacks because clothing did not always fit into the budget of her poverty-stricken family. Today, Forbes estimates Winfrey's net worth at $3 billion

At the age of six years, she was sent north to join her mother and two half-brothers in a Milwaukee ghetto, which was an extremely poor and unsafe area. At the age of twelve, she was sent to live with her father in Nashville, Tennessee. Here she felt secure and happy. For a brief period, she began making speeches at social gatherings and churches, and once she even earned five hundred dollars for a speech. It was then that she decided that she wanted to be 'paid to talk'.

She was raped for the first time at age 9 by her 19-year-old cousin, writes Oscar Bamwebaze Bamuhigire in his book *'The Healing Power of Self Love'*. It would be the first of several episodes. At age 14, Winfrey broke free and went to live with her dad in Nashville, Tennessee, where her success would start to take course.

Her father saved her life. He was very strict and provided her with guidance, structure, rules and books.

She was raped for the first time at the age of 9 by her 19-year-old cousin, writes Oscar Bamwebaze Bamuhigire in his book 'The Healing Power of Self Love'.

He wanted her to complete weekly book reports. She went without having dinner until she had learned five new words each day. Oprah was an outstanding student, contributing as well in the drama club, debate club and student council. In an Elks Club speaking competition, she won a complete scholarship to Tennessee State University. The next year she was invited to a White House Session on Youth. She was crowned Miss Fire Prevention by WVOL, a local Nashville radio station, and was hired by the station to read afternoon newscasts.

She became the first black female news anchor before the age of 20 in Nashville, starting with a few gigs as a local anchor before landing a co-anchor position in Baltimore. She was sexually harassed and humiliated at her job in Baltimore, according to Daily Worth, but didn't need to quit—she was fired seven and a half months after joining. Winfrey didn't stay down for long. She landed a gig hosting the then-stagnant morning talk show, 'AM Chicago'.

Oprah moved to Chicago, Illinois, in January 1984 and took over as presenter on A.M. Chicago, a morning talk show that was steadily last in the ratings. She altered the emphasis of the show from old-style women's issues to contemporary and contentious topics, and after one month, the show was even with Donahue's programme. Three months later, it had crept ahead. In September 1985, the programme, renamed the Oprah Winfrey Show, was expanded to one hour. As a result, Donahue moved to New York City.

Oprah was an outstanding student, contributing as well in the drama club, debate club and student council. In an Elks Club speaking competition, she won a complete scholarship to Tennessee State University.

She made a savvy, career-transforming move in 1986 when she founded Harpo Productions and negotiated ownership of the 'The Oprah Winfrey Show', which brought in $300 million a year during its peak. Her company later produced lucrative spinoff shows, including 'Dr. Phil' and 'Rachael Ray'.

The popularity of her show rose steeply after the feat of *The Color Purple*, and in September 1985, the distributor King World subscribed the rights to distribute the television programme to air in 138 cities. This was a record for any show. That year Winfrey won the top ten markets in the United States.

In 1986, she won an exceptional award from the Chicago Academy for the Arts for unique contributions to the city's artistic community and was named Woman of Achievement by the National Organization of Women. The Oprah Winfrey Show won several Emmys for Best Talk Show, and Winfrey was honoured as Best Talk Show Host.

Though best known for her talk show, Oprah has also been involved in movies, television series and plays. She was nominated for an Academy Award for Best Supporting Actress for her performance in the 1985 drama *'The Color Purple'*. She also published her own magazine, The Oprah Magazine; started a radio channel, Oprah Radio; and most recently partnered with Discovery Communications to launch a cable channel, the Oprah Winfrey Network.

Today she ranks among the highest paid TV personalities in the world and owns a lavish lifestyle. She is surely one of the names history would remember for eternity.

❑

The Celebrity Next Door

Oprah started her broadcasting job at WVOL radio in Nashville while still in high school. At the age of 19, she became the youngest person and the first African-American woman to anchor the news at Nashville's WTVF-TV. She then moved to Baltimore's WJZ-TV to co-anchor the 'Six O'Clock News' and later went on to become co-host of its local talk show, People Are Talking.

For decades, she has been so well known that people hardly use her last name. Her large fortune makes her the richest celebrity in the United States. With an income of several million dollars per year just from television, she is the highest paid television persona. In the Harris poll

Oprah started her broadcasting job at WVOL radio in Nashville while still in high school. At the age of 19, she became the youngest person and the first African-American woman to anchor the news at Nashville's WTVF-TV.

for five years in a row, she was chosen as the favourite television star. Her annual viewership average is 7.3 million. In spite of plentiful competitors, her daily television show has continued to be on the top of daytime programmes.

Once in December 1983, Oprah was in Baltimore to host a local daytime talk show. She was wearing a fur coat, and what she called her 'big mama earrings'. Waving to people along State Street, she yelled, 'Hi, I'm Oprah Winfrey. I'm the new host of A.M. Chicago .... Miss Negro on the air'. During her first week, the local morning show crushed the countrywide popular 'Donahue show' in the ratings. A year later, Phil Donahue, the major of talk show television, was forced to change his time slot, so as not to compete with Oprah's show. By now Oprah had received a $1 million signing bonus and her show was sold in 138 markets. During that first year, she became an instant sensation and went on to appear on The Tonight Show, won two local Emmys and was to make her movie debut in

The Color Purple. Her role as Sofia in that film brought her a huge fan following and also brought her the Golden Globe and the Oscar nominations for Best Supporting Actress.

Once in December 1983, Oprah was in Baltimore to host a local daytime talk show. She was wearing a fur coat, and what she called her 'big mama earrings'.

Oprah spent the summer of 1985 filming the movie. She later recalled, '*The Color Purple* was the first time I ever remember being in a family of people where I truly felt loved ... when people genuinely see your soul and love your soul, when they love you for who you are and what you have to give'. She continued, 'I was destined for great things'. She also said, 'I'm Diana Ross, and Tina Turner, and Maya Angelou'.

A week before the movie's premiere, she decided to do a show on rape, incest and sexual molestation. The station agreed reluctantly. It ran announcements seeking volunteers to talk about their sexual abuse on television. The show became Oprah's signature style – a victim who conquests hardship – and the fight of the Oprah Winfrey sensation.

On Thursday, 5 December 1985, the show began with the introduction of a young white woman who identified herself as Laurie. 'One out of three women in this country

A week before the movie's premiere, she decided to do a show on rape, incest and sexual molestation. The station agreed reluctantly. It ran announcements seeking volunteers to talk about their sexual abuse on television.

have been sexually abused or molested', she told the audience. 'Your father started fondling you. When did it lead to something other than fondling?' 'I think around between nine and ten', said Laurie. 'What happened? Do you remember the first time your father had sexual intercourse with you? What did he say to you, how did he tell you, and what did he tell you?' There was not a sound from the audience of mostly white women. 'He just told me that he wanted to make me feel good', said Laurie. 'Where was your mother?' 'She had gone on a trip somewhere—she was out of town. She was gone for three weeks and I stayed with my father for those three weeks'.

'So he came into your room ... and he started fondling you. That has to be a pretty frightening thing when you're nine years old and your father has sexual intercourse with you'. Laurie nodded but said nothing. 'I know it's hard to tell—I really do. I know how hard it is. When he was finished, what did he—or during this act—well, first of all, wasn't it painful for you?' Laurie squirmed a bit. 'Um.

He used to tell me that he was sorry and that he would never do it again. A lot of times after he would do something, he would kneel down and make me pray to the Lord and say that he wouldn't do it anymore'. Moments later Oprah waded into the audience and planted her microphone in front of a middle-aged white woman in glasses. 'I was sexually abused, too', the woman said. 'Well, my life kind of started like Laurie's with the fondling and ... It resulted in a child who's now—he's thirty years old right now, but sixteen years of his life he's been in a state institution [for autism]'. 'Were you sexually abused by a member of your family?' The woman choked up as she admitted being impregnated by her father. 'So this is your father's child?' said Oprah. 'Yes. It happened very frequently—as with Laurie also—practically every day when my mother would go to work. One of the most horrible experiences that I can remember'.

Moments later Oprah waded into the audience and planted her microphone in front of a middle-aged white woman in glasses. 'I was sexually abused, too', the woman said.

As Laurie broke down, Oprah spread her arm around her and then burst into tears herself. She sobbed into the woman's shoulder. 'The same thing happened to me', she said.

Her confession made nationwide news, and she was celebrated by many for her uprightness and candour. But her family fervently repudiated her charges.

Produced by Oprah's Harpo Studios, The Oprah Winfrey Show amused, educated and uplifted millions of viewers for next 25 years. It reached more than 40 million viewers a week in the United States as the top-rated talk show and was permitted in 150 countries internationally.

Products advertised by Oprah became a big hit. Anything she ate, drank or wore reaped much profit from the Oprah linking. Green tea, a specific diet or a distinct type of brassiere, when advertised by Oprah, become immediate best-sellers. On one of her shows, she presented Susan Nethero, chief artist and creator of a group of lingerie shops. Participants and Oprah herself were fitted with their bras. At the end of the show, Oprah announced she finally got the right size. The company gained P.R. that led to the opening of more shops. Sales of merchandises presented on the show, which provides to a typically female audience, become astral.

In 2008, Oprah and Discovery Communications publicized plans to make OWN: Oprah Winfrey Network, the first and only network named for, and inspired by, a single iconic leader. Oprah's heart and creative instincts inform the brand – and the magnetism of the channel. Oprah provided leadership in programming and attracted superstar talent to join her in primetime, building a global community of like-minded viewers and leading that community to connect on social media and beyond. OWN is a joint venture between Harpo, Inc. and Discovery Communications. The network debuted on 1 January 2011 and is available in 85 million homes. The venture also includes the award-winning digital platform Oprah.com. Effective from July 2011, Oprah assumed the positions of Chairman, Chief Executive Officer and Chief Creative Officer for the network.

A poll taken in 2008 at Sacred Heart University found a sudden decline in Oprah's popularity. More than half of the respondents were not in favour of her involvement with public policy. It was attributed to her participation in the presidential race of 2008 and her support of the Obama campaign. Harsh attacks against Oprah began once her support for Obama was announced and continued after the Republican convention. Also, many feminists felt betrayed because she'd chosen Obama over Hillary Clinton.

Despite all the controversies assigned to her name, she remains one of the most iconic celebrities of our times.

❑

The Girl Called Oprah

In 1992, she hosted a documentary called Scared Silent: Exposing and Ending Child Abuse. It became the most-watched documentary ever in the history of national television. In the year 1993, she also started lobbying for the National Child Protection Act. The act went on to establish a database of sentenced child abusers and was known by the name Oprah Bill. Regrettably, the law was not effective. It was supposed to provide information gathered from all states about sex convicts and fierce criminals to groups working with children. Most of the states did not set up the measures for the groups to apply for background

In the year 1993, she also started lobbying for the National Child Protection Act. The act went on to establish a database of sentenced child abusers and was known by the name Oprah Bill.

checks, and, according to a June 2006 report by the U.S. Attorney General, the Oprah Bill did not have the envisioned influence. Years down the line, she created Oprah's Child Predator Watch List at the website www.oprah.com, to help track down child sex offenders. By December 2005, there were more than ten men on the list, and then fifteen months later, five of them could be arrested as Oprah drew attention to their cases. She even went to the extent of offering to reward with an amount of $100,000 for the information leading to the arrest of any of the men on the list, and by September 2008, nine of those men were captured. Oprah kept her word and paid out $100,000 to those who turned the men in. All through her television career, she persistently did shows on sexual abuse. Many of them were complimentary ('I Want My Abused Kids Back', 'Call Girls and Madams', 'Fathers Dating Their Daughters' Friends' and 'Women Who Turn to Lesbianism'), others were groundbreaking ('Sexual Abuse in Families', 'Rape and Rape Victims' and 'How to Protect Yourself from Abduction by a Rapist').

Oprah Winfrey is known throughout the world for her philanthropic, educational and social work. In the aftereffects of Hurricane Katrina in New Orleans, Oprah's aid was written about in papers everywhere. She donated $10 million for hurricane relief.

Oprah Winfrey is known throughout the world for her philanthropic, educational and social work. In the aftereffects of Hurricane Katrina in New Orleans, Oprah's aid was written about in papers everywhere. She donated $10 million for hurricane relief. She also gave gifts to volunteers who helped after the disaster. She called her celebrity friends to help her bring attention the plight. Infuriated, she used her show to apologize in the name of the American people for the suffering and deaths that had taken place. She asked viewers to donate money. Her appeal helped raise $15.6 million. With the amount raised, more than 300 new houses were built or refurbished. The project work took place in eight communities in Oprah's home state of Mississippi as well as Texas, Louisiana and Alabama. Her relief programme provided new books to thousands of children who had lost their books in the tragedy.

Although not well known for its cultural life, Mississippi is Oprah's birthplace. She was born in a little-known area of Mississippi called Kosciusko. The city was named after the Polish general Thaddeus/Tadeusz Kosciusko.

Although not well known for its cultural life, Mississippi is Oprah's birthplace. She was born in a little-known area of Mississippi called Kosciusko. The city was named after the Polish general Thaddeus/ Tadeusz Kosciusko. Known as the 'Hero of Two Worlds', he fought for the independence of the colonies in the American Revolution as well as for the independence of his home country. Much admired for his abilities, he also served with the Continental Congress, which appointed him an engineer with the rank of colonel. Kosciusko is only 70 miles north of the capital city, Jackson, but there is almost no similarity between the two places. Little differentiates Kosciusko from other small farming areas of the state, yet during America's early years, it was a vital part of the border route to Nashville. People in those days used the

In April 2002, Oprah launched the first international edition of O, The Oprah Magazine, in South Africa, extending her 'live your best life' message to another broad audience.

Mississippi River whenever possible to transport goods, a method that was often problematic for primitive navigation.

During the 20th century, Southern states – Georgia, Louisiana, Tennessee, Alabama and Virginia – proved to be more fruitful ground than Mississippi for writers, novelists and essayist. Oprah, on her shows and in her interviews, often speaks of the books that moved her the most during her growing up days. Many of her favourite books are the ones written by southern writers, traditional and contemporary poets, literary critics, novelists, playwrights and essayists.

The peculiar aspect of the books of these writers is the great cultural chasm between the races and also the similarities within each racial group. The Black writers educate the reader about the suffering and oppression caused by white people. When, in adulthood, Oprah and some of her friends have spoken of these matters. Their words reflect the books, poems and stories that are part of the

United States' literary and cultural heritage. Oprah and her friends have lived these stories.

Oprah lived in two Southern states, Mississippi and Tennessee. She spent a few childhood and teenage years in Milwaukee, Wisconsin, and in her 20s moved to Maryland. Ultimately, Chicago became her primary home.

In April 2000, Oprah and Hearst Magazines introduced O, The Oprah Magazine, and a monthly magazine that has become one of today's leading women's lifestyle publications. It is credited as being the most successful magazine launch in recent history and currently has a circulation of 2.35 million readers each month. In April 2002, Oprah launched the first international edition of O, The Oprah Magazine, in South Africa, extending her 'live your best life' message to another broad audience.

The story of Oprah Winfrey, a poor, fatherless black child, neglected by her teenage mother, came before the world when she started giving interviews. 'I never had a store-bought dress', she told a group of reporters, 'or a pair of shoes until I was six years old.... The only toy I had was a corn cob doll with toothpicks...'. In her interviews, she recalls her childhood years as lonely, with no one to play with except the pigs. In one such interview, she claimed, 'I had only the barnyard animals to talk to.... I read them Bible stories. We were so poor we couldn't afford a dog or cat, so I made pets out of two cockroaches.... I put them in a jar, and named them Melinda and Sandy'.

She entertained her viewers with stories of carrying water from the well. 'I used to get thrashing all the time from my grandmother. It's just part of Southern tradition—the way old people raised kids. You spill something, you get a whipping; you tell a story, you get a whipping.... My grandmother whipped me with switches.... She could beat me every day and never get tired'.

Oprah lived in two Southern states, Mississippi and Tennessee. She spent a few childhood and teenage years in Milwaukee, Wisconsin, and in her 20s moved to Maryland. Ultimately, Chicago became her primary home. Oprah attended high school and college in Tennessee. At the time of her birth in 1954, the jobs were scarce, and young people, particularly young blacks, continued to be victims of prejudice and poverty.

❑

Troubled Childhood

Oprah credits her maternal grandmother, Hattie Mae Lee, and her father, Vernon Winfrey, for her success, but the memories of her childhood are filled with pain and sadness.

She was born illegitimate, the child of two young people. Her mother, Vernita Lee, at age 18 claimed that a 20-year-old man named Vernon Winfrey, a soldier stationed at Camp Rucker in Alabama, on leave for two weeks from the army was the father of her child.

The baby was named Oprah. It was a biblical name from the book of Ruth. Sometime later, Vernita left her

Oprah credits her maternal grandmother, Hattie Mae Lee, and her father, Vernon Winfrey, for her success, but the memories of her childhood are filled with pain and sadness.

infant with her mother, Hattie Mae. Oprah spent her early years with her grandmother. Till the age of six, she lived on a little farm with her grandmother in the Mississippi Delta region. Later she went to live with her mother in Milwaukee, Wisconsin.

Life on the farm was difficult. Since the family had no washing machine, water had to be drawn from a well. She had to help with the cows, pigs and chickens. She slept with her grandmother. Grandfather used to threaten her with his cane and so did her grandmother. In one of her interviews, she recalls 'the reason I wanted to be white was that I never saw little white kids get whippings, I used to get them all the time from my grandmother. It's just part of Southern tradition—the way old people raised kids. You spill something, you get a whipping; you tell a story, you get a whipping.... My grandmother whipped me with switches.... She could beat me every day and never get tired'.

Hattie Mae Lee often took Oprah to nearby Faith-United Mississippi Baptist Church. She was taught how to read and to memorize passages of the Bible. Thanks to her ability to recite pieces from the Bible, she was called on to do Easter selections. 'I would just get up in front of her friends and start doing pieces I had memorized', Oprah once said. 'Everywhere I went, I'd say, "do you want to hear me do something?"'

Hattie Mae Lee often took Oprah to nearby Faith-United Mississippi Baptist Church. She was taught how to read and to memorize passages of the Bible. Thanks to her ability to recite pieces from the Bible, she was called on to do Easter selections.

Her religious fervour in childhood brought her the hostility of other youngsters who gave her the nicknames 'The Preacher' and 'Miss Jesus'. By age of seven, she developed a taste for inspirational poems such as William Ernest Henley's 'Invictus'. On her grandmother's farm, she was lonely, sequestered and friendless. She grudged white children, whose families owned television sets and washing machines, who were not punished for every little misdeed. 'The reason I wanted to be white was that I

Oprah's mother, Vernita, lacked the qualities of her own mother. She had no room in her apartment for a six-year-old Oprah.

never saw little white kids get whippings', she told writer Lyn Tornabene.

Oprah's only friends were the pigs she helped take care of. She would read, talk and tell stories to them. By the time she was six, she began looking forward to living with her mother in Milwaukee. Life at the farm with her grandmother taught her to be strong, spiritual and a believer in God. The time also helped her ability to reason and gain her sense of self and the feeling of obligation to help others.

Oprah's mother, Vernita, lacked the qualities of her own mother. She had no room in her apartment for a six-year-old Oprah. She managed her household with the help of welfare money and the earnings that she made by cleaning houses. She also had a third illegitimate child when Oprah was about nine years old. Oprah was unwanted, and a burden in the house. She was treated inferior to her half-sister whose skin was lighter in comparison to hers. The owner of the house, Mrs. Miller, praised the younger child to Oprah. 'Mrs. Miller [the landlady] did not like me because of the color of my skin', Oprah recalled. 'Mrs. Miller was a light-skinned black woman who did not like darker-skinned black people. And my half-sister [was] light-skinned, and she was adored. It was not something that was ever said to me, but [it was] absolutely understood that she is adored because she is light-skinned and I am not'.

From an early age, like any African Americans, Oprah has been conscious of colour. 'White people never made me feel less', she said years later. 'Black people made me feel less. I felt less in that house with Mrs. Miller. I felt less because I was too dark and my hair was too kinky.... I felt like an outcast'. When she got into college, she became cynical, about the kinds of colour discrimination practiced not only on the outside but also within the black community.

Long after her college years were behind her, she continued to speak of blacks as being 'fudge brownies'. Once talking about Harold Washington, the city's first African-American mayor, she said 'We're fudgies. There are fudgies, gingerbreads and vanilla creams. Gingerbreads are the ones who, even though you know they're black, have all the features of whites.... Vanilla creams are those who could pass if they wanted to, and then there's folks like me and the Mayor. No mistakin' us for anything but fudgies'.

Her favourite books during her college days were the ones written on racial issues: slavery; segregation, violence

A year after Oprah moved to Milwaukee to be with her mother, Vernita had a third child, Jeffrey Lee, on 14 December 1960. After Jeffrey's birth, she moved into the small apartment of her cousin Alice Cooper and lived for a while on welfare.

against blacks – rape, lynching and other forms of murder; injustice and the legal system; and discrimination in all its varieties.

Her reading and acting preferences interlocked in 1985 when Quincy Jones, a casting director, asked her to play the role of a character named Sofia in a movie about African Americans, based on Alice Walker's book, *The Color Purple*. The movie went on to become a huge success.

A year after Oprah moved to Milwaukee to be with her mother, Vernita had a third child, Jeffrey Lee, on 14 December 1960. After Jeffrey's birth, she moved into the small apartment of her cousin Alice Cooper and lived for a while on welfare. She sent Oprah to live with Vernon Winfrey, her biological father in Nashville.

In comparison to the life that she lived at her grandmother's farm, life with her was comparatively a big low for her. It was only later in her career that she realized this fact. However, after moving under her fathers' custody, her life took the turn that she needed the most.

Oprah was sent to live with her father and stepmother, Zelma, in Nashville, Tennessee. They were happy to have the 7-year-old living with them because they could not have children of their own. Finally, Oprah could enjoy the experience of having her very own bed and bedroom. Vernon lived in a little brick house on Owens Street in East Nashville and worked for Vanderbilt University as a janitor. He welcomed Oprah and gave her a proper home with structure – schooling, regular visits to the library, a little bit of television, playtime and church every single Sunday. Oprah was enrolled in Wharton Elementary School and allowed to skip a grade once again. The third grader was thrilled that her parents took her to the library and valued her education. The family attended church regularly, and Oprah found more opportunities for public speaking, even at this young age.

Oprah was enrolled in Wharton Elementary School and allowed to skip a grade once again. The third grader was thrilled that her parents took her to the library and valued her education.

Vernita promised Oprah all the television she wanted in Milwaukee, and, ironically, it was that little bribe that led to a life-changing moment for her daughter.

Since Vernon and Zelma had no children of their own, they wanted to raise Oprah themselves. Strongly religious, Vernon Winfrey was very active in his church, Faith United, and he saw to it, as Grandmother Lee had, that Oprah attended all services and youth-oriented activities. The Winfrey home was rigorously run, a place where learning for a child was central, and Zelma, known as a strict disciplinarian, required Oprah to read a certain number of books on a regular basis, write, learn math and develop a strong vocabulary.

After Zelma died, Vernon remained a widower for several years until he met the woman who became his second wife.

Oprah used to spend the end of the summer with Vernita because her mother was going to get married. Besides, Oprah's life with 'Daddy' and 'Mama Zelma' in Nashville had been a bit too restricted, with only an hour of television a day, and never on Sundays. Vernita promised Oprah all the television she wanted in Milwaukee, and, ironically, it was that little bribe that led to a life-changing moment for her daughter. 'I stopped wanting to be white when I was ten years old and saw Diana Ross and The Supremes perform on The Ed Sullivan Show', Oprah said. 'I was watching television on the linoleum floor in my mother's apartment [on a Sunday night]…. I'll never forget it…. It was the first time I had ever seen a colored person wearing diamonds that I knew were real…. I wanted to be Diana Ross…. I had to be Diana Ross'.

Vernon Winfrey wasn't happy about having his daughter go back to the environment of Vernita's household. Oprah experienced reversion in the congested, hearsay, unruly life she'd led before, only worse.

After completing third grade, Vernon took his daughter back to Milwaukee to visit her mother. In the time since Oprah left, Vernita had given birth to a baby boy named Jeffrey. The three children shared a room in the family's two-bedroom apartment. Vernon returned in the fall to take Oprah back to Nashville, but she chose to stay with her mother and began the fourth grade in Milwaukee. In her mother's absence, Oprah turned to the television for company and had her first thoughts of being famous one day.

Vernon Winfrey wasn't happy about having his daughter go back to the environment of Vernita's household. Oprah experienced reversion in the congested, hearsay, unruly life she'd led before, only worse. She soon became the frequent object of sexual abuse. After being raped by a cousin at an uncle's house when she was nine, over the next five years she experienced molestation that she has described as unending and persistent until she went to live again in her father's home. She was abused by numerous men, among them other relatives and her mother's boyfriends. When she was first raped by her cousin, she says, she didn't understand what had happened, particularly when the cousin convinced her not to tell by bribing her with an ice cream cone and a trip to the local zoo.

When, at the age of 14, she told her mother about the abuse, she denied her statement that a brother of his had been one of the perpetrators. Her mother's refusal to discuss the matter was so traumatic that Oprah never brought it up again with her.

Vernon and Zelma sent Oprah to East Wharton Elementary School in Nashville. Her fourth-grade teacher named Mrs. Duncan inspired her so much that for a time she wanted to become a teacher. When she lived with her mother for the second time, she did very well at the

Lincoln Middle School, located in the poor inner city of Milwaukee. Oprah got help from a teacher, to change to Nicolet, a newly integrated Milwaukee high school. Gene Abrams, one of Oprah's teachers at the new school, took notice of her love for reading. He took the time to help her transfer to an all-white school in Glendale, Wisconsin. Later Oprah said that she was the only one in her class selected for that honour. 'I was in a situation where I was the only black kid, and I mean the only one, in a school of two thousand upper-middle-class suburban Jewish kids. I would take the bus in the morning to school with the maids who worked in their homes. I had to transfer three times'.

Gene Abrams, one of Oprah's teachers at the new school, took notice of her love for reading. He took the time to help her transfer to an all-white school in Glendale, Wisconsin.

The year Oprah began attending Nicolet High was the same year when both Martin Luther King, Jr., and Robert Kennedy were assassinated. 'In 1968 it was real hip to know a black person, so I was very popular. The kids would all bring me back to their houses, pull out their Pearl Bailey albums, bring out their maid from the back and say, 'Oprah,

Vernon Winfrey was rigid about grades, persistently expecting that she earn A's. However, he never rewarded her for any achievements. Zelma, his wife, also wanted Oprah to do all the things necessary to become an outstanding student.

do you know Mabel?' They figured all blacks knew each other. It was real strange and real tough', she says.

At the age of 14 she began to skip school, date boys, steal money from her mother and even run away. Vernita could not handle this behaviour for long, so Oprah was sent back to Nashville to live with her father.

Vernon started to change Oprah into a 'proper young lady'. 'Every morning of my life my step-mother would check me out to make sure I'd picked out the right socks, that everything matched', she told in a TV interview. 'When I weighed 70 pounds I had to wear a girdle and a slip every day. God forbid somebody should see through your skirt! What are they going to see? The outline of your leg, that's all!' 'When it came to discipline, hard was the only way I knew', Vernon said years later. 'My own daddy could wring a hoot from the mourners' bench', Vernon said, '[but] Oprah had a way of keeping my blood up. If I pulled east, she'd tug west. If I pointed north, she was hell-bent on south. She wasn't an unpleasant child. In fact, her company was a great joy to me. But she did have a problem with directions'. Oprah was put to work in the small grocery store that Vernon operated next to his barbershop. 'I hated working in that store', Oprah said, 'hated every minute of it'. During the autumn of 1968, she started school as a sophomore at East Nashville High. She went unnoticed for most of her first year. She attended class every day but sat quietly in the back.

> *I wasn't the kind of kid who would persist in telling until someone believes you. I didn't think enough of myself to keep telling'.*

Vernon Winfrey was rigid about grades, persistently expecting that she earn A's. However, he never rewarded her for any achievements. Zelma, his wife, also wanted Oprah to do all the things necessary to become an outstanding student.

Soon she had realized that she was pregnant. She decided to hide this news from her parents. When her legs and ankles swelled and her belly bulged, her stepmother took her to a doctor. She was pregnant. 'Having to go home and tell my father was the hardest thing I ever did', Oprah continues, 'I wanted to kill myself'. She told her father that his brother could be her child's father. 'Everybody in the family sort of shoved it under a rock', Oprah told Ebony 's Laura Randolph. 'Because I had already been involved in sexual promiscuity they thought if anything happened, it had to be my fault and because I couldn't definitely say that he was the father of the child, the issue became "Is he the father?" not the abuse.... I wasn't the kind of kid who would persist in telling until someone believes you. I didn't think enough of myself to keep telling'. She went into early labour on the same day she told her father about the pregnancy. She delivered a baby boy, who died within two weeks. It was premature and ill. After being kept him in an incubator for one month and eight days, the baby died. Because of being psychologically unsound, Oprah never got to see her child.

❑

The Transformation

After the horror of pregnancy, Oprah decided to bring her life on track. She started attending school again. A change came about for 16-year-old Oprah when she first read Maya Angelou's autobiography, 'I Know Why the Caged Bird Sings'. It transmuted her outlook, and she later said, 'I read it over and over, I had never before read a book that validated my own existence'.

After entering Nashville's East High School, she became very active. She was chosen as vice president of her class and president of the student council, drama club and National Forensics League. At school, Oprah joined the National Forensic League and worked closely with

At school, Oprah joined the National Forensic League and worked closely with Ms. Haynes on dramatic interpretations to prepare for competitions. The goal was to win the Tennessee State Forensic Tournament and qualify for the nationals.

Ms. Haynes on dramatic interpretations to prepare for competitions. The goal was to win the Tennessee State Forensic Tournament and qualify for the nationals. During her time at the school, she was chosen for membership in the National Forensic League. In 1971, she was chosen to attend a White House Conference on Youth. 'I went back to school and not a soul knew. Nobody', she told in 2007. 'Otherwise, I would not have had this life that I've had'.

She began her broadcasting career at WVOL radio in Nashville while still in high school. Upon her return from the White House conference in Colorado, Nashville's WVOL radio station requested an interview with her. Shortly after the interview, impressed by her articulate voice and flamboyant style, she asked to work for the station. Shortly after Oprah started working part-time, the station, black-operated and with a primarily black audience, wanted somebody to represent it in the contest of Miss Fire

Prevention. The Miss Fire Prevention competition was a beauty contest in which every girl except Oprah was white. First asked what she'd do with the money if she won, she told the judges she'd be a 'spending fool'. And when asked about her wishes for a future career, she said she wanted to be a journalist in the broadcasting. Oprah won, becoming the first black girl to be named Miss Fire Prevention. Following this, she became the first Miss Black Nashville in a pageant, and later, in another beauty contest, she was named Miss Black Tennessee and she won a trip to Hollywood.

In 1971, after graduating from high school, she went on to Tennessee State University. Colour discrimination had dominated her life. It even dictated her college choice.

Oprah's first experience in journalism came from WVOL radio station. After the beauty pageant, she accepted an offer to hear her voice on tape. This led to a part-time position reading the news. At the age of 19, she became the youngest person and the first African-American woman to anchor the news at Nashville's WTVF-TV. She then relocated to Baltimore's WJZ-TV to co-anchor the 'Six O'Clock News' and later went on to become co-host of its local talk show, People Are Talking.

In 1971, after graduating from high school, she went on to Tennessee State University. Colour discrimination had dominated her life. It even dictated her college choice.

In 1970, she was one of twelve finalists at a public-speaking competition sponsored by the Black Elks Club of Nashville, a service organization formally known as the Improved Benevolent Protective Order of Elks of the World. 'I can't remember what I said but my topic was "The Negro, The Constitution, and The United States". I delivered it in front of 10,000 people in Philadelphia and I felt really comfortable up there. I had always worried whether my slip was hanging down whenever I got up to speak but in front of 10,000 people you realize nobody can see if it's hanging down. You can't get scared when it's a sea of people everywhere you look'. Oprah won the competition at the Seventy-first Grand Lodge Convention, which honoured Mayor Charles Evers of Fayette, Mississippi, with its highest award, a four-year college scholarship.

In 1971, after graduating from high school, she went on to Tennessee State University. Colour discrimination had dominated her life. It even dictated her college choice. She enrolled at Tennessee State University, a historically black college in Nashville, rather than the private, more prestigious Fisk University. It was during her time at TSU that she participated in the prestigious Miss Black beauty pageant. Although a runner up in the contest, she managed to leave a deep impression on the judges and the audience. At TSU, she majored in speech and language arts.

Hired at $150 a week, Oprah made her television debut in Nashville in January 1974. By the following year, she had received several awards as the city's first black female on television.

After the college, she started working full time at the radio stations. Reading the weekend news, and, later, making occasional broadcasts during the week, she made $100 a week.

Later, she was offered an opportunity with a radio station called WLAC. Soon she moved to its television channel, WLAC-TV, as a reporter and co-anchorperson, the first woman as well as the first black person to hold that position. Hired at $150 a week, Oprah made her television debut in Nashville in January 1974. By the following year, she had received several awards as the city's first black female on television. She was named National Executive Woman of the Year by the National Association of Women Executives. The Middle Tennessee Business Association named her Outstanding Businesswoman of the Year, and

Oprah got dumped in 1977, eight months after she had joined. She was no longer a star. While her contract guaranteed twenty-five more months of pay, she had no standing at the station.

she won the Negro Business and Professional Women's Club award as Woman of the Year in 1975. As the thirtieth-largest television market, Nashville was a training ground for many young broadcasters like Oprah.

In the 1970s, local news became a big moneymaker for television, especially in Baltimore, where Jerry Turner anchored on WJZ-TV every night. In 1976, the station decided to go to an hour news format and announced search for a co-anchor to share stage with Turner. At the time there were only a few black women on television in Baltimore, despite the city's large black population. It was at this point that Oprah emerged in the scene. She was ill at ease, and her unexperienced background led to awkward blunders. It became apparent very quickly that Oprah wasn't meant to be a newswoman. She was too emotional to be a reporter and would get carried away and react to the human aspects of all situations. 'It was a great way of introducing me to the city. I probably know more about the neighborhoods now than anybody else at the station', she says.

Oprah got dumped in 1977, eight months after she had joined. She was no longer a star. While her contract guaranteed twenty-five more months of pay, she had no standing at the station. Yet she couldn't quit, because she needed the money. So she picked up any assignment that came her way. In addition to doing the local cut-ins for Good Morning America, she became a weekend feature reporter. She was demoted from her evening anchor position, but a new station manager found her a slot with co-host Richard Sher on a morning programme called People Are Talking. Since she enjoyed doing a talk show, she stayed with the job for several years.

In 1984, Oprah moved to Chicago to host WLS-TV's morning talk show, AM Chicago, which became the number one local talk show—surpassing ratings for Donahue—just one month after she began. In less than a year, the show expanded to one hour and was renamed The Oprah Winfrey Show. It entered national syndication in 1986, becoming the highest-rated talk show in television history. In 1988, she established Harpo Studios, making her the third woman in the American entertainment industry (after Mary Pickford and Lucille Ball) to own her own studio. She remained in Chicago for more than 25 years before moving to California.

❑

The Oprah Winfrey Show

'I remember coming home from high school as a teen to watch Oprah. She taught us a lot about what women experience. It was quite informative. We loved her'.

– Anonymous

Chicago's television viewers were new to a black, overweight woman doing the daily talk show, and they were loving this new experience. Accustomed to the cerebral style of the other talk show hosts, the crude larks of Oprah Winfrey were a shock. Unlike other daytime offerings, the show was completely unrehearsed and extemporaneous. 'I usually don't do homework', said Oprah. 'I really have learned that for me and my style of interviewing, the less preparation I do, the better because what everybody is now calling Oprah's success is me being spontaneous and that's all it is'. Never overwhelmed by success, Oprah was always confident, especially after her rival TV show host Donahue moved from Chicago to New York City.

Accustomed to the cerebral style of the other talk show hosts, the crude larks of Oprah Winfrey were a shock. Unlike other daytime offerings, the show was completely unrehearsed and extemporaneous.

If one counts the number of times one particular theme that has been used on her show, obesity would be the winner. She on her show often talks about the importance of exercise and organization, whereas she talks about writing thoughts in a journal so that the temptation to overeat can be tackled. She got her first national publicity in Newsweek, when she deposed Phil Donahue in the ratings. She was thrilled to get a full page in the national newsmagazine.

In no time Oprah became an immediate sensation in Chicago. People on the street would run into restaurants just to watch her eat. She was soon the most sought-after celebrity in the town. Her success came at a time when shows like Geraldo Rivera's 'trash TV' dominated the ratings. But her show was something different. It was compassionate,

> *In no time Oprah became an immediate sensation in Chicago. People on the street would run into restaurants just to watch her eat. She was soon the most sought-after celebrity in the town.*

empathetic and uplifting. The qualities became to be associated with the show as it grew. Her celebration of life was a way to connect to everyone, and it finally went on to define daytime TV in the 90s.

It was Oprah's ability to find something in each story that her audience could relate with. From setting aside audience by eye colour in a 1992 show to help people understand the experiences of racism, to discussing her own history of childhood sexual abuse, Oprah made everything so personal that the viewers could not help but fall in love with her.

The show, over its course, also became the platform for celebrities to show the side of theirs that the audience were often unaware of. For example, Tom Cruise on the show discussed his relationship with Katie Holmes, and Michael Jackson revealed about his Neverland ranch to debunk rumours about his life. And the most popular of them all was when cyclist Lance Armstrong publicly confessed to doping that he had denied for years. Among other celebrities whose appearance with Oprah caught the attention of television journalists was the Olympic champion figure skater, Oksana Baiul, because of her disagreement with Oprah about drinking. Not everyone featured on the show was a celebrity, though.

Among other celebrities whose appearance with Oprah caught the attention of television journalists was the Olympic champion figure skater, Oksana Baiul, because of her disagreement with Oprah about drinking

Strewn with straightforward or expressive topics are some unusual admissions. For example, a recent subject was husbands who have sex changes. The episode showed the many characteristics of Oprah's presentations that account for her large numbers of viewers. Her natural ability lies at rapport talk, something that is typical of women's conversations. During an episode shot on 11 January 1995, she broke down and made the scandalous confession: 'I did your drug', to a mother who was talking about her addiction to crack cocaine. 'It's my life's great big secret that has always been held over my head', she continued.

Oprah became the first black woman to successfully host her own daytime talk show on national television, although Della Reese had hosted a daytime variety show

The Oprah Winfrey Show entertained its millions of viewers for 25 years. The show reached more than 40 million viewers a week in the United States as the top-rated talk show and was licensed to 150 countries internationally.

from 1969 to 1970. Oprah reached at a time when African Americans were at last succeeding on the air. As a black female, she profited from favourable action, but she also brought a huge flair to her place at the table. She identifies herself as a woman first and then as a black woman, but not as a black spokeswoman.

The Oprah Winfrey Show entertained its millions of viewers for 25 years. The show reached more than 40 million viewers a week in the United States as the top-rated talk show and was licensed to 150 countries internationally. After a 25-year run, show's finale was heralded by a two-part episode filmed in Chicago's United Center with over 13,000 audience members and celebrities like Beyoncé and Aretha Franklin bidding her farewell. The last episode took place inside the studio on 25 May 2011 and was attended by Morehouse students who were recipients of a scholarship she helped raising money for.

As far as her future endeavour in television is concerned, her website says:

'In 2008, Oprah and Discovery Communications announced plans to create OWN: Oprah Winfrey Network, the first and only network named for, and inspired by, a single iconic leader. Oprah's heart and creative instincts inform the brand—and the magnetism of the channel. Oprah provides leadership in programming and attracts superstar talent to join her in primetime, building a global community of like-minded viewers and leading that community to connect on social media and beyond. OWN is a joint venture between Harpo, Inc. and Discovery Communications. The network debuted on January 1, 2011 and is available in 85 million homes. The venture also includes the award-winning digital platform Oprah.com. Effective July 2011, Oprah assumed the positions of Chairman, Chief Executive Officer and Chief Creative Officer for the network.

Oprah provides leadership in programming and attracts superstar talent to join her in primetime, building a global community of like-minded viewers and leading that community to connect on social media and beyond.

Oprah's Lifeclass is a true multi-platform experience with millions of students from over 200 countries around the world engaging with Oprah on-air, online and via social media. In the popular series, Oprah and handpicked experts interact with fans worldwide in inspiring conversations about principles that guide our lives. The series, which is also live streamed at Oprah.com and Facebook, features a digital classroom with course work to accompany episode themes'.

❑

Oprah and the Movies

Everybody loves and recognizes Oprah Winfrey from her long-running, record-breaking, daytime television talk show called 'The Oprah Winfrey Show'. But apart from her television projects, she has also produced, starred in and voiced characters in movies on the big and small screens.

Here's a list of some of her performances and projects she has been a part of.

The Color Purple – 1985: This movie was based on the 1982 novel by Alice Walker named '*The Color Purple*'. It launched not only her acting career but along with her, the careers of Whoopi Goldberg and Danny Glover. It was directed by Stephen Spielberg, and Winfrey often mentioned on her popular daytime talk show that she did all that she could in her power to win the role of Sophia.

She was also nominated for the Academy Award for Best Supporting Actress for her performance in this movie. She later went on to produce the Broadway version of '*The Color Purple*' in NYC, starring Jennifer Hudson.

Native Son - 1986: This was her second film role. Oprah starred in this 1986 film named 'Native Son', which had a cast consisting Matt Dillon, Elizabeth McGovern and Victor Love.

The film follows the story of Bigger Thomas, a man who takes a job as a chauffeur at a rich family. After an unlucky chain of actions, Bigger unintentionally kills his employer's daughter and tries to cover it up by putting the blame on her boyfriend in order to protect himself from the biased trial he discerns he would get as an African-American man in 1940s' Chicago.

Beloved - 1998: It was in 1998 that Oprah's dream of having the critically acclaimed Toni Morrison novel 'Beloved' appear on the big screen came true. Coming together with Danny Glover, her co-star from '*The Color Purple*', the two played Sethe and Paul. The characters of Denver and Beloved portray Morrison's story of dependence, expense and progress that was brought to the crowds. Though the movie was praised by the critics, it did not prosper as premeditated at the box office.

Their Eyes Were Watching God - 2005: This movie was based on Zora Neale Hurston's 1937 novel by the same name. This movie tells the story of a free-spirited woman named Janie Crawford. It was produced by Oprah's Harpo Productions and starred Academy Award winner Halle Berry.

Charlotte's Web - 2006: The movie featured Oprah's voice along with those of Julia Roberts, Steve Buscemi, John Cleese, Dakota Fanning, Kathy Bates and Robert Redford in the film. The movie was based on the children's novel of the same name.

Oprah lent her voice to the character named Gussie the Goose in the barn where the much loved Wilbur the pig and Charlotte the spider hatch their plan to keep Wilbur off the family's dinner plate. This film was Oprah's first work as a voice artist.

Bee Movie - 2007: In the 2007 animated movie named 'Bee Movie', which starred the voices of Jerry Seinfeld, Renee Zellweger and Matthew Broderick, Oprah played the role of Judge Bumbleton. This movie followed the story of Barry B. Benson (Seinfeld), a bee, as he sued the world for honey theft with the help of his human companion Vanessa Bloome (Zellweger) and best friend Adam Flayman (Broderick). Her voice and popularity were used in the movie as she went on to portray the judge in the case of Benson vs. the world.

The Princess and the Frog - 2009: This 2009 movie named 'The Princess and the Frog' starred Oprah as the voice of Eudora, mother of the main character Princess Tiana. This Disney movie was a return to the hand-drawn animation that followed the story of a young princess in New Orleans and her experiences with a frog prince.

❑

A Day in the Life of Oprah

Fans of Oprah are always curious to know what it is like waking up every morning as Oprah. Oprah, though, lives a fairly simple life. Surprised? Read to find out more.

Oprah-Style Summer

Nothing fancy. Summer for Oprah is sleeping a little later, reading a little longer and calling an old friend for a spur-of-the moment lunch. Outside in the garden, frogs croaking and crickets chirping. Summer means fresh fruit and vegetables, and Oprah salads. It's time for long hikes, and basking under the sun on a beautiful rocking chair placed on the front porch. It is time to sit down with a glass of rosé at the end of the day. It is a call to senses – particularly of pleasure.

The not so Glamorous Life

She is very close to her dogs who greet her in the morning by jumping on her bed. This is their way of letting her know that they are ready for a walk. Hence, her day begins with poop patrol.

A Good Start

Sometimes on a summer morning, Oprah meditates by the pool. And the meditation is often accompanied with reading of the newspaper. This is how she tunes in to herself, and then simultaneously to the world.

Cheap Thrills

After the newspaper, it's time for the breakfast. Breakfast is often either a green smoothie or a boiled egg with baby spinach and avocado, followed by a mug of chai.

Earthly Delights

'I've never planted a lettuce I didn't like. In Chicago, I'd toss leftover greens, but when I grow something, I feel an obligation to either eat it or share it with the neighbors. You get such an abundance of produce from even the tiniest little plot. Every leaf of kale is a thrill, so why not spread the joy?' says Oprah.

It is at her garden that she whiles away her time taking candid pics with her beloved gardener on her iPhone.

The Daily Schedule

'My first breath as I am coming out of sleep is always a thank you!' says Oprah Winfrey when asked about her daily schedule. Given below is a piece from her daily routine.

6:00 a.m. Oprah never sets an alarm, she doesn't believe in them. For her alarms are ...; alarming! And she puts the number in her mind and wakes up before that, usually sometime between 6:02 and 6:20, because her dogs are trained to go out at that time. She hops up, brushes her teeth and takes the dogs to do their thing. She prepares a chai tea or skim cappuccino and put on her sneakers.

'Yesterday I got up at 6. I was going to get up at 5:30, but at 1 a.m. I sent an e-mail to security saying, "Give me an extra half hour". I got to the office about 6:30 and got on the treadmill downstairs in the gym. While on the treadmill I play Scrabble on my iPad, against the computer', said Oprah.

7:30 a.m. She goes to the gym downstairs in her house by the time 'Eye Opener' hits on CBS. She checks out what Gayle [King] is wearing on 'Eye Opener'! She has a fantastic Octane elliptical machine which is like a power mover — one can increase the length of their stride and arm movement. She does 20 minutes on the elliptical and 30 minutes walking on the treadmill. Then she starts out at the Level 3 incline setting and then every minute she adds to the incline until she gets to 12 or 15. And then she does sit-ups.

8:00 a.m. She does some form of walking or sitting meditation. She likes to sit in a window seat in her house or outside on the balcony. If she is in a hotel, she would simply sit in a chair. If she has the time, she would do 20 minutes; if she is in a rush, she'll do 10 to 12 minutes. She eats medium-boiled eggs and a piece of multigrain toast for breakfast. Oprah has actually noticed that lately she has been eating breakfast at 8:38. And then she takes some vitamin D.

9:00 a.m. She goes through her schedule during breakfast. She has phone calls and video conferences, does her bank wires, business transactions and financial stuff. She tries to get all of that done by noon or 12:30 when she is at home, since that's 3 p.m. in New York and the banks close soon after that.

11:30 a.m. 'I drink a green drink—spinach, parsley, a little bit of apple juice, celery, and cucumbers in a blender—and made some phone calls. I had to call Africa, and you have to do that before everybody goes to bed over there', says Oprah.

12:35 p.m. 'I got back in the makeup chair—I was running late—and then did a show with Barbra Streisand', says Oprah.

1:00 p.m. Lunch sometimes gets moved back because of the morning, but she likes to eat at around 1. She would have soup and a big salad. Usually the salad is made with vegetables that come from her garden. She has a rule in her house: If she can grow it, she doesn't buy it. She uses everything in the garden, even if it means she is giving it to the people down the street.

2:00 p.m. After that, she has the rest of her day. When she gets off the phone, she has a video conference with her team about the marketing of Greenleaf [OWN's drama series on which Winfrey has a regular acting role], and she will get on the phone with creator Craig Wright in the writers room. She will have a conversation later on with Ava DuVernay, as currently she is shooting 'A Wrinkle in Time', about Queen Sugar.

'I came back upstairs, called the bank with any transfers that needed to be made, money issues. Then we had meetings about the next week's shows, what we have coming up', says Oprah.

6:00 p.m. Oprah likes to have dinner by 6 or 6:30 if she is home alone. She often cooks for Stedman Graham, Winfrey's longtime boyfriend and herself, but she doesn't cook for more than four people. She doesn't measure things when she cooks, she sort of makes it up as she goes along, hence it is hard for her to figure out if she is feeding more than four. Sometimes she has guests too, like a bunch of girls on break [they are graduates of the Oprah Winfrey Leadership Academy in Johannesburg, South Africa, who now go to college in the United States]. So the chef cooks for in such situations. She always does a protein, two vegetables and a carb. Oprah does a carb because if she tries to just do protein and veggies, her body thinks that she is trying to make it diet and then she ends up eating three times the amount of Weight Watchers points, as she is trying to satisfy herself not having the carb. So she does a rice or pasta or polenta or something. Her protein is usually fish or some form of grilled or baked chicken.

7:50 p.m. 'Yesterday was an early day, since I was on the treadmill again by 10 of 8. I'd already done 45 minutes in the morning, so I did 30 minutes. Actually, it took 34 minutes to finish my Scrabble game, and I stayed on to 35 to round it off. The guy next to me was at a level-50 incline, and I was at 10. I was embarrassed to stay at 10, so I moved to 20. I was like panting—but I was going to keep it there', says Oprah.

8:00 p.m. She likes to wind down for the night by the fire. She has a fire going in every fireplace during night! And she reads to relax. These days she is reading *'The Hour of Land'* by Terry Tempest Williams. And she is loving it so much that she thinks her new thing is going to be seeing as many of the national parks as she can. She might make a bucket list and put that on there. At this time, she also reads scripts that come in.

8:50 p.m. 'This almost never happens, but I came home at the same time as Stedman Graham, Oprah's longtime love. I made him something for dinner—leftover shrimp and rice, a little salad with lettuce, olive oil. I shaved some truffles, chopped up rosemary, I made it for him. I had a rice cake with almond butter. I'm trying not to eat past 7:30. I sat at the kitchen table and we talked for maybe 30 minutes, then I went to bed', Oprah says.

10:00 p.m. By this time she usually gets into bed and she has volumes and volumes of gratitude journals by the side of her bed. The last thing she does before she goes to sleep is write five things that gave her great pleasure or that she was grateful for.

'I took my little stack of books to bed. I was trying to figure out what the next book club selection was going to be'. She chose *Great Expectations* and *A Tale of Two Cities*.

11:10 p.m. 'Lights out'.

5 Morning Rituals of Oprah Winfrey:

Success asks one to get up early. Much can be achieved within the first few hours before the dawn as morning rituals can set one up for success in life. As a matter of fact, some business leaders accomplish more in the first few hours than many average persons like us would do so in days. Oprah's example of using those few hours and making sure that they count can be a source of inspiration to many.

Before Oprah goes on to face the hustle and bustle of her tough and cruel world, she makes sure that she rests her mind for at least 20 minutes through deep meditation.

Meditation

Before Oprah goes on to face the hustle and bustle of her tough and cruel world, she makes sure that she rests her mind for at least 20 minutes through deep meditation. This power of meditation should not be undermined as several other successful and celebrated personalities like Arianna Huffington and Russell Simmons are fans of this practice too. When Oprah, after one of her morning sessions of meditation, was asked to comment on it she said, 'I walked away feeling fuller than when I'd come in. Full of hope, a sense of contentment, and deep joy. Knowing for sure that even in the daily craziness that bombards us from every direction, there is—still—the constancy of stillness. Only from that space can you create your best work and your best life'.

Exercises

Oprah says that she hits the treadmill in her gym to sweat it out every morning. Exercise in its own way has a key to helping many successful people to keep their daily productivity and energy level always up. And no doubt that this proves to be highly beneficial if they are having a rough day at work.

It's Time to Tune In

Each has his/her own way of tuning him/herself to becoming the best they can be. It could be simply listening to one's favourite song, or it could also be going out for a walk, or preparing a delicious meal. For Oprah, she tunes herself in for her day by playing scrabble on her new iPad, even while she walks or jogs or works it out on the treadmill.

Oprah Eats Healthy

While many would eat fatty foods that would quickly burn out and leave them feeling fatigued, Oprah prefers to eat a healthy meal every day. Her meal is made out of carbohydrates, a lot of fibre and of course protein. This could be anything, from drinking a green drink, which is a combination of parsley, a little bit of apple juice, celery, and cucumbers in a mixer; to having her ceremonial tea or chai.

Oprah Gets to Work

Oprah does what she loves and she does so as early as possible in the morning. She would often record two shows in the morning.

So this is how Oprah starts her day.

❑

Oprah and Controversies

With a great public life come great controversies. During her long career of more than 25 years, Oprah has had plenty of them. Here's a list of some of her most prominent controversies.

Oprah vs. Sarah Palin

When Sarah Palin was selected as John McCain's vice presidential pick in the 2008 campaign, Oprah's fans and her staff suggested that she call Palin on her show. But Oprah during the campaigns had publicly endorsed Barack Obama for the post of president, and hence refused to use her programme as a political platform for candidates.

When Sarah Palin was selected as John McCain's vice presidential pick in the 2008 campaign, Oprah's fans and her staff suggested that she call Palin on her show.

The Republican Party was furious, disagreeing, saying that it was a hypocritical decision on Oprah's part. Although Obama had appeared on her show back in 2006. But Oprah pointed out that it was before he announced his candidacy for the president. Several gossip magazines and news organizations claimed that political inclination was the reason behind Oprah's decision of not having the first woman running on a Republican ticket on her show as a guest. On 16 November 2009, Palin finally appeared on the show to discuss her memoir Going Rogue.

Oprah vs. Beef

Throughout the time period of the mad-cow scare in 1996, Oprah, on her show, invited a cattle rancher-turned vegetarian, named Howard Lyman, to discuss the contentious observations in the beef industry, which also included the process called 'rendering', which is now banned in the United States. The practice involves turning organs of a cow into the fodder for other cattle. Winfrey though argued against some of Lyman's more bizarre declarations—

like the suggestion that the disease could become as contagious as AIDS—she cried after the show that such exposes had stopped her from eating beef. This caused the beef prices to plunge for next two weeks after the episode aired. The prices reached a 10-year low. Oprah was sued by Texas cattle farmers. Her comments were thought to have seriously influenced her viewers to turn away from eating beef. She was sued for $10.3 million by the farmers. The jury found Winfrey was not liable for damages. 'Free speech not only lives, it rocks', Oprah told reporters in February 1998. 'I'm still off hamburgers', she added.

In 1996, Oprah, on her show, invited a cattle rancher-turned vegetarian, named Howard Lyman, to discuss the contentious observations in the beef industry, which also included the process called 'rendering', which is now banned in the United States.

Oprah vs. Iraq War

Although Oprah endorsed her political affiliations publicly only with the candidacy of Barack Obama, which also drew widespread media attention, she had dipped her toe into political waters before. During plenty of episodes aired in November 2002 and through the spring of 2003,

During plenty of episodes aired in November 2002 and through the spring of 2003, Oprah talked openly of the side effects of potential U.S. action against Saddam Hussein in Iraq.

Oprah talked openly of the side effects of potential U.S. action against Saddam Hussein in Iraq. It was the time when the talks and demands for war were growing louder with every passing day. However, Oprah chose to play off this news and went on to schedule a two-day special, 'The World Speaks Out on Iraq', for the day after Secretary of State Colin Powell's crucial speech before the United Nations in February 2003. Despite the fact that the episodes drew praise from antiwar section among the audience, several government officials showed discontent over the episodes. There was conjecture that the Bush Government deliberately scheduled a press session with the President and Powell during Winfrey's show so that her anti-war message could be downplayed.

Oprah and 'The Secret'

The next controversy hit her door when she chose to publicly praise the best-selling self-help book *The Secret*, written by new age guru Rhonda Byrne. But by promoting it consecutively on the two episodes of her show, she ran into trouble. The book's main theme is that positive thinking is the route to obtaining what one wants in life, and the negative thoughts will lead to bad events. Soon the producers of the show got a letter from a viewer named Kim Tinkham. She was undergoing a breast-cancer diagnosis sometime after the episodes aired. Tinkham had decided to abandon chemotherapy, and instead chose to follow the advice given in the book. Oprah called Tinkham on the show to make her understand the advantages of medical science. Tinkham, went on to follow another book called the *pH Miracle*, died in December 2010.

On 22 June 2005, Oprah was denied entrance to the Hermès luxury store in Paris. Hermès staff failed to recognize her and asked her to leave.

Oprah vs. Letterman

'Could you tell me please what has transpired?' Oprah asked during her December 2005 appearance on the Late Show with David Letterman. This was an attempt to set matters straight between the two. When Letterman hosted the 1995 Academy Awards, he made the corny 'Uma, Oprah' joke. He ostensibly introduced Winfrey to Uma Thurman. He also called the 'Oprah Log', in which he kept a daily diary of whether or not he had been invited

Oprah decided to make Pieces an official book club selection in 2005 and the paperback version immediately shot to the top of the New York Times' bestseller list for 15 straight weeks.

to appear on her show. This incident affected Winfrey the wrong way. In a 2003 interview with *TIME*, Oprah said 'I felt completely uncomfortable' as the target of his jokes. The two decided to finish the feud, and in the 2005 meeting, Oprah appeared on Letterman's show before the premiere of the Broadway version of *The Color Purple*.

Oprah and the Crash

On 22 June 2005, Oprah was denied entrance to the Hermès luxury store in Paris. Hermès staff failed to recognize her and asked her to leave. After her fans began shunning the store, Oprah decided to clear the situation by addressing her audience. She said that though the store was close to closing, there were apparently customers inside. She called the experience 'humiliating' and called the experience a similar one for any person 'who has ever been snubbed because you were not chic enough or thin enough or the right class or the right color'. The store's president Robert

Chavez appeared on the show to publicly apologize to Oprah.

Oprah vs. James Fray

When James Frey presented his book *'A Million Little Pieces'* to Oprah, she was touched by Frey's supposedly true story of substance abuse and redemption. Oprah decided to make *Pieces* an official book club selection in 2005 and the paperback version immediately shot to the top of the New York Times' bestseller list for 15 straight weeks. Later, it emerged that the supposed-autobiography was in fact much more fiction than fact. In January, the Smoking Gun published a detailed account of the book's inaccuracies, including the fact that Frey never served jail time, as he claims in the book. Embarrassed, Oprah then invited Frey onto the show and took him down several pegs. 'I have to say it is difficult for me to talk to you', she told Fray. Frey explained himself that the drug addiction

Oprah decided to make Pieces an official book club selection in 2005 and the paperback version immediately shot to the top of the New York Times' bestseller list for 15 straight weeks.

led him to lie in his writing. Oprah sternly chided Frey, 'I feel you betrayed millions of readers'. Oprah also brought his editor Nan Talese onto the show. 'I really feel duped', Nan Talese admitted. Frey's literary agent dropped him, and his two-book deal was voided.

Oprah and the Doctor

Oprah's 7 million daily viewers are given a number of health tips. While guests offer advice on eating and fitness, the show many times becomes a scene for some dubious medical claims. As Newsweek noted, actress Jenny McCarthy on Oprah's show linked well-known vaccines to autism—with hardly any challenge from Oprah. Suzanne Somers and Robin McGraw endorsed on the show a hormone therapy for women. It has been claimed that the therapy can also boost the risk of heart attacks and strokes. Observers question Oprah's enthusiasm for novel cosmetic surgery procedures, which occasionally lead to unwelcome complications down the road.

There have been several rumours regarding Oprah's sexuality since 1997. In 1997, she appeared on Ellen DeGeneres show where she revealed to the world that she was gay.

Oprah and the Rumours

There have been several rumours regarding Oprah's sexuality since 1997. In 1997, she appeared on Ellen DeGeneres show where she revealed to the world that she was gay. At that time she had recently broken off with Stedman Graham and rumours that Oprah and Gayle King were a couple began doing the rounds. Oprah denied the claims in a 2006 O Magazine interview. Like Oprah, King has repeatedly dismissed the claims too.

When Oprah picks a book for the Oprah's Book Club segment on her show, 'the Oprah Effect' takes place, and sales of the book usually spike by million copies.

Oprah and the Scandal in South Africa

At the time when the Oprah Winfrey Leadership Academy for Girls opened in Johannesburg in 2007, Nelson Mandela, Tina Turner, Sydney Poitier, Spike Lee and Oprah herself attended an extravagant ribbon-cutting ceremony. The motive was to celebrate the landmark boarding school, founded with $40 million of Oprah's money. But only a year later, six of the 152 students selected by Oprah to study at the institution came out in public accusing dorm matron Virginia Tiny Makgobo of sexual and physical abuse. 'It has shaken me to my core', Oprah said. 'This has been one of the most devastating, if not the most devastating, experiences of my life', she continued.

Oprah vs. Jonathan Franzen

When Oprah picks a book for the Oprah's Book Club segment on her show, 'the Oprah Effect' takes place, and sales of the book usually spike by million copies. When Oprah chose Franzen's sweeping 2001 family drama *'The Corrections'* as a club selection, the author stiffened. He didn't feel that his work belonged in the company of the other selections, lamenting, 'The problem in this case is some of Oprah's picks. She's picked some good books, but she's picked enough schmaltzy, one dimensional ones that I cringe, myself, even though I think she's really smart and she's really fighting the good fight'. Moreover, he also was at discomfort for having the Oprah's Book Club logo on the novel's cover. Franzen later backed off from his earlier comments, in which he had advocated being picked by Oprah would put men off reading his book, and thanked her for her interest in the book.

Oprah vs. Ludacris

When Ludacris appeared on Oprah's show in 2006, Oprah chastised him for using the words 'bitches' and 'ho's' in his songs. Ludacris was shocked by the interview, which he claimed continued even after the show went off the air. He then accused Oprah of editing out his replies. He told media, 'Of course, it's her show, but we were doing a show on racial discrimination, and she gave me a hard time as a rapper when I came on there as an actor. It was like being at someone's house who doesn't really want you there'.

Oprah vs. Angelina Jolie

Oprah's recent project is the Oprah Winfrey Leadership Academy for Girls in South Africa. The boarding school is devoted to finding academically gifted low-income girls in South Africa and then nurturing their leadership abilities. Oprah looks to other celebrities for help with promoting the school. Oprah invited Angelina to lend a hand in promoting the school. Jolie supposedly flatly refused. She was seemingly still riled that Oprah had sided with Jennifer Aniston in Aniston's breakup with Jolie's beau Brad Pitt.

❑

Filmography

Producer (41 credits)

- 2016–2018 Greenleaf (TV Series) (executive producer – 42 episodes)
- 2012–2018 Oprah's Master Class (TV Series documentary) (Executive Producer – 43 episodes)
- 2017 The Immortal Life of Henrietta Lacks (TV Movie) (Executive Producer)
- 2016–2017 Queen Sugar (TV Series) (executive producer – 29 episodes)
- 2016 First Lady Michelle Obama Says Farewell to the White House: An Oprah Winfrey Special (TV Special) (executive producer)

- 2014–2016 Super Soul Sunday (TV Series) (executive producer - 6 episodes)
- 2015 Oprah Goes to Broadway: *The Color Purple* (Executive Producer)
- 2015 Oprah's Master Class: Belief Special (TV Movie) (Executive Producer)
- 2015 Oprah's Master Class: Civil Rights Special (TV Movie documentary) (Executive Producer)
- 2014 Selma (Producer)
- 2014 The Hundred-Foot Journey (Producer)
- 2012 Oprah and Rainn Wilson Present SoulPancake (TV Special) (Executive Producer)
- 2012 Oprah's Master Class: Special Edition (TV Movie) (Executive Producer)
- 2012 Oprah's Next Chapter (TV Series) (Executive Producer)
- 2011 Serving Life (TV Movie documentary) (Executive Producer)
- The Oprah Winfrey Show (TV Series) (Supervising Producer - 9 episodes, 1989–2011)
- 2011 Extraordinary Moms (TV Movie documentary) (Executive Producer)
- 2011 Your OWN Show (TV Series) (Executive Producer)

- 2010 The Oprah Winfrey Oscar Special (TV Special) (Executive Producer)
- 2009 Christmas at the White House: An Oprah Primetime Special (TV Special) (Executive Producer)
- 2009 Precious (Executive Producer)
- 2008 Every Monday Matters (Video documentary short) (Executive Producer)
- 2007 The Big Give (TV Series) (Executive Producer)
- 2007 The Great Debaters (Producer)
- 2007 Mitch Albom's For One More Day (TV Movie) (Executive Producer)
- 2007 Building a Dream: The Oprah Winfrey Leadership Academy (TV Movie documentary) (Executive Producer)
- 2007 The Oprah Winfrey Oscar Special (TV Movie) (Executive Producer)
- 2006 Legends Ball (TV Movie documentary) (Executive Producer)
- 2005 Their Eyes Were Watching God (TV Movie) (Executive Producer)
- 2002 Oprah After the Show (TV Series) (Executive Producer)
- 2001 Amy & Isabelle (TV Movie) (Executive Producer) / (Producer)
- 1999 Tuesdays with Morrie (TV Movie) (Executive Producer)

- 1998 David and Lisa (TV Movie) (Executive Producer)
- 1998 The Wedding (TV Movie) (Executive Producer)
- 1997 Before Women Had Wings (TV Movie) (Producer)
- 1993 Michael Jackson Talks to... Oprah Live (TV Special) (Executive Producer)
- 1993 ABC Afterschool Specials (TV Series) (Producer – 1 Episode)
- 1992 Overexposed (TV Movie) (Executive Producer)
- 1992 Nine (TV Movie documentary) (Executive Producer)
- 1989 The Women of Brewster Place (TV Series) (Executive Producer – 2 Episodes)
- Actress (27 credits)
- 2018 A Wrinkle in Time (Post-Production)
- 2017 The Star (Completed)
- Deborah (Voice)
- Richard Pryor: Is It Something I Said? (Announced)
- Terms of Endearment (Film Series)
- 2016-2017 Greenleaf (TV Series)
- 2017 The Immortal Life of Henrietta Lacks (TV Movie)
- 2014 Selma
- 2013 Making a Scene (Short)
- 2013 The Butler
- 2011 Jesus Henry Christ

- 2010 Si Agimat at si Enteng Kabisote
- 2010 Sesame Street (TV Series)
- 2009 The Princess and the Frog
- Eudora (Voice)
- 2008 30 Rock (TV Series)
- 2007 Bee Movie
- Judge Bumbleton (Voice)
- 2006 Charlotte's Web
- Gussy the Female Goose (Voice)
- 2005 Desperate Housewives: Oprah Winfrey is the New Neighbor (TV Short)
- 1999 Our Friend, Martin (Video)
- Coretta Scott King (Voice)
- 1998 Beloved
- 1997 Before Women Had Wings (TV Movie)
- 1997 Ellen (TV Series)
- 1992 Lincoln (TV Movie)
- Elizabeth Keckley (Voice)
- 1990 Brewster Place (TV Series)
- 1986 Native Son
- 1985 *The Color Purple*
- Soundtrack (3 credits)

- 2004-2010 The Oprah Winfrey Show (TV Series) (Performer – 2 Episodes)
- 1998 Beloved (performer: 'Sethe's Lullaby', 'Pullin' The Skiff')
- 1987 Dolly (TV Series) (Performer – 1 Episode)

❑

Honours and Achievements

Oprah during her elaborate career has earned a number of achievements and honours. Some of them are the following:

2013:

❖ Recipient of the Presidential Medal of Freedom.

2012:

❖ Spelman College—National Community Service Award.

2011:

❖ The Board of Governors of the Academy of Motion Picture Arts and Sciences—Jean Hersholt Humanitarian Award/Honorary Academy Award.

- National Academy of Television Arts & Sciences—Crystal Pillar Award.
- *TIME* Magazine—100 Most Influential People in the World. She is the only person to have been included in all eight of TIME'S 100 Most Influential People in World lists, from 2004 to 2011.

2010:

- The John F. Kennedy Center for the Performing Arts—Kennedy Center Honors.
- The Women's Conference (California)—Minerva Award.

2007:

- The Elie Wiesel Foundation for Humanity—2007 Humanitarian Award.

2006:

- The New York Public Library—Library Lion 2006.

2005:

- National Association for the Advancement of Colored People—Hall of Fame.
- National Civil Rights Museum—2005 National Freedom Award.
- International Academy of Television Arts & Sciences—2005 International Emmy Founders Award.

2004:

- United Nations Association of the United States of America—Global Humanitarian Action Award.
- National Association of Broadcasters—Distinguished Service Award.

2003:

- Association of American Publishers—AAP Honors Award.

2002:

- 54th Annual Primetime Emmy Awards®—Bob Hope Humanitarian Award.
- Broadcasting & Cable—Hall of Fame.

1999:

- National Book Foundation—50th Anniversary Gold Medal.

1998:

- National Academy of Television Arts & Sciences®—Lifetime Achievement Award.
- The following year, after accepting this highest honour, Oprah removed herself from future Emmy® consideration and the show followed suit in 2000. Oprah and The Oprah Winfrey Show received more than 40 Daytime Emmy Awards®: seven for Outstanding Host; nine for Outstanding Talk Show; more than 20 in the Creative Arts categories; and one for Oprah's work as

supervising producer of the ABC After School Special Shades of a Single Protein.

- TIME Magazine—100 Most Influential People of the 20th Century.

1997:

- Newsweek—Most Important Person in Books and Media.
- TV Guide—Television Performer of the Year.

1996:

- International Radio & Television Society Foundation—Gold Medal Award.
- George Foster Peabody Awards—1995 Individual Achievement Award.

❑

Success Principles of Oprah Winfrey

In the world of media, Oprah Winfrey has established an unparalleled connection with the people around the world. She, as a host and supervising producer of the award-winning The Oprah Winfrey Show, has entertained, enlightened and uplifted millions of viewers worldwide for more than 25 years. Her endeavors as a global media trailblazer and philanthropist have proven her as one of the most esteemed and respected public figures today.

Winfrey Gail Winfrey was born to Vernita Lee and Vernon Winfrey on a remote farm in Kosciusko, Mississippi, on January 29, 1954. Her parents decided to name her Orpah from the Bible, but because of the trouble of spelling and articulation, she has been called Oprah all her life. Her bachelor parents parted soon after she was born and left her in the upkeep of her maternal grandmother on the farm.

Winfrey Gail Winfrey was born to Vernita Lee and Vernon Winfrey on a remote farm in Kosciusko, Mississippi, on January 29, 1954. Her parents decided to name her Orpah from the Bible, but because of the trouble of spelling and articulation, she has been called Oprah all her life.

As a child, Oprah Winfrey wore potato sacks because clothing did not always fit into the budget of her poverty-stricken family. Today, Forbes estimates Winfrey's net worth at $3 billion, and she is the only black woman on the publication's list of the 400 wealthiest people in America.

During her childhood, she entertained herself by play-acting in front of an audience of farm animals. Underneath the strict supervision of her grandmother, she learned to read at two and a half years old. She lectured her church audience about "when Jesus rose on Easter Day" when she was two years old. Then she hopped kindergarten after lettering a note to her teacher on the first day of school, saying she fitted in the first grade. Winfrey's school promoted her to third grade after that year.

She became the first black female news anchor before the age of 20 in Nashville, starting with a few gigs as a local anchor before landing a co-anchor position in Baltimore. She was sexually harassed and humiliated at her job in Baltimore

Before she became a media mogul and the queen of daytime TV, Winfrey suffered a tumultuous childhood. She was shuffled between family members, spending her first few years on her grandmother's farm in rural Mississippi. At the same time, her unwed teenage mom looked for work, according to the Academy of Achievement.

At the age of six years, her family members sent her north to join her mother and two half-brothers in a Milwaukee ghetto, which was an impoverished and unsafe area. At the age of twelve, her mother sent her to live with her father in Nashville, Tennessee. Here she felt secure and happy. For a brief period, she began making speeches at social gatherings and churches, and once she even earned five hundred dollars for an address. It was then that she decided that she wanted to be "paid to talk."

She was raped for the first time at age nine by her 19-year-old cousin, writes Oscar Bamwebaze Bamuhigire in his book *"The Healing Power of Self Love."* It would be the first of several episodes. At age 14, Winfrey broke free and went to live with her dad in Nashville, Tennessee, where her success would start to take the course.

She made a savvy, career-transforming move in 1986 when she founded Harpo Productions and negotiated ownership of the "The Oprah Winfrey Show," which brought in $300 million a year during its peak.

Her father saved her life. Often he was very strict and providing her with guidance, structure, rules, and books. He wanted her to complete weekly book reports. She went without having dinner until she had learned five new words each day. Winfrey was an outstanding student, contributing as well in the drama club, debate club, and student council. In an Elks Club speaking competition, she won a full scholarship to Tennessee State University. The next year she was invited to a White House Session on Youth. She was crowned Miss Fire Prevention by WVOL, a local Nashville radio station, and was hired by the station to read afternoon newscasts.

She became the first black female news anchor before the age of 20 in Nashville, starting with a few gigs as a local anchor before landing a co-anchor position in Baltimore. She was sexually harassed and humiliated at her job in Baltimore, according to Daily Worth, but didn't need to quit - she was fired seven and a half months after joining. Winfrey didn't stay down for long. She landed a gig hosting the then-stagnant morning talk show, "AM Chicago."

Winfrey moved to Chicago, Illinois, in January 1984 and took over as presenter on A.M. Chicago, a morning talk show that was steadily last in the ratings. She altered the emphasis of the show from old-style women's issues to contemporary and contentious topics, and after one month, the show was even with Donahue's program. Three months later, it had crept ahead. In September 1985, the program, renamed the Oprah Winfrey Show, was expanded to one hour. As a result, Donahue moved to New York City.

She made a savvy, career-transforming move in 1986 when she founded Harpo Productions and negotiated ownership of the "The Oprah Winfrey Show," which brought in $300 million a year during its peak. Her company later produced lucrative spinoff shows, including "Dr. Phil" and "Rachael Ray."

The popularity of her show rose steeply after the feat of *The Color Purple*. In September 1985, the distributor King World subscribed the rights to distribute the television program to air in one hundred thirty-eight cities. Such kind of subscription was a record for any show. That year Winfrey won the top ten markets in the United States.

In 1986 she won an exceptional award from the Chicago Academy for the Arts for unique contributions to the city's artistic community. She was named Woman of Achievement by the National Organization of Women. The Oprah Winfrey show won several Emmys for Best Talk Show, and Winfrey was honored as Best Talk Show Host.

Though best known for her talk show, Winfrey has also been involved in movies, television series, and plays. She was nominated for an Academy Award for Best Supporting Actress for her performance in the 1985 drama *"The Color Purple."* She also published her magazine, The Winfrey Magazine, started a radio channel, Winfrey Radio, and most recently partnered with Discovery Communications to launch a cable channel, the Oprah Winfrey Network.

Today she ranks among the highest-paid T.V. personalities in the world and owns a lavish lifestyle. She is undoubtedly one of the names history would remember for eternity.

She has proved her mettle in the world of media. She has been a constant in the list of the most influential people around the world. Her rags to riches story inspire many youngsters to follow their passion.

She has proved her mettle in the world of media. She has been a constant in the list of the most influential people around the world. Her rags to riches story inspire many youngsters to follow their passion. Her ability to pick impactful stories and to take them to the living rooms of the people around the world has made her a household name in America and Europe. She comes from humble beginnings. But she never allowed her lack of privilege to stop her from pursuing her dreams and ultimately fulfill them.

Let's have a look at some of her life mantras:

1. **Craft your art:** You must become skilled and vigilant at what you do. Never allow others to stop you from believing in yourself. Always remember the promise you made to yourself when you were young. Hone your skills and take every step to fulfil your childhood promise. You are only on this planet to be you, not someone else's imitation of you. In Winfrey's 20s, when she first started broadcasting, she was just pretending to

be Barbara Walters. She was just trying to talk, act, and behave like her. Due to this imitation, she faced many embarrassing moments during her live broadcasting. Once, when she was going to broadcast news, and she hadn't read the copy due to which she miss pronounced the word Canada. It was very embarrassing for her because she was live on air at that time and she cracked herself up because she thought that the previous host would never miss pronouncing that word. And that little moment stopped her from pretending and allowed the real her to come through. Your life journey is about learning to become more of who you are and fulfilling the highest and most authentic expression of yourself as a human being. That's why you are here on this planet.

2. **Find a way to serve:** We must find a way to help. Martin Luther King said that not everybody could be famous, but everybody can be great because greatness is determined by service. We live in a world where everybody wants to be recognized and where we admire people for just being famous. We think being known brings us value. The truth is all of that will fade in time. The real truth is that the service and significance that you bring to your job is what lasts forever. Never forget that we all owe in different measures to society. Therefore all of us strive to give back to the community. Use your knowledge and talent in service to the world if you look at the most successful people in the world,

whether they know it or not they have that paradigm of service. They do service to the world and then become prosperous. Winfrey decided that she was no longer going to just be on T.V, but she was going to use it as a platform and as a force for some excellent service and not be used by T.V.

3. **Take responsibility:** You are responsible for your life, and if you are sitting around waiting on somebody to save you from your problems or to help you fix it, you are wasting your time, because only you have the power to take responsibility to move your life forward. The sooner you get that, the faster your metabolism gets into gear. What matters now is to live in the present. You need to be aware of your surroundings and must be willing to see this moment for what it is. Accept the present, forgive the past, take responsibility, and move forward.

4. **Always do the right thing:** Be excellent so that people notice. Make yourself noticeable to others. If you do the right thing, people will see you. Excellence shows itself, be unique. Let your distinction be your brand. Everybody talks about building a brand, but Winfrey never knew what that was. When people say you are a brand, she would say, "No, I am just Winfrey." But what she recognizes now is that her choice in every experience to do the right thing is what has created the brand. When you are excellent, you become

unforgettable; people remember you, and you stand out from the rest of the crowd. We all want to be memorable. Doing the right thing even when nobody knows it will always bring a good result to you. This is true because the third law of motion is still at work, i.e., every action has an equal and opposite reaction, and that is at work at every moment of our lives.

5. **Listen to the universe:** Universe speaks to us. It is always communicating. It does so through whispers. At first, such hints in your life feel odd, or they don't make any sense. The sound gets louder with every passing moment, but if we fail to pay attention to it, then it gradually becomes subtle. Ultimately it fades away. As Oprah says, Life whispers to you all the time. It whispers, and if you don't get the whisper, the whisper gets louder. If you don't get the whisper when it gets louder, I call it like a little pebble—a little thump—upside the head. The pebble or the thump upside the administrator usually means it's gone into a problem. If you don't pay attention to the problem, the stone then becomes like a brick. The brick upside your head is a crisis, and If you don't pay attention to the block upside your head, the crisis turns into a disaster, and the whole house—brick wall—comes falling." Catch up the whisper and listen to the universe.

6. **Become the best version of yourself:** Winfrey has always paid attention to her life because she knows that

her life is still speaking to her just like any other person. It will take some time to understand it, but once you start paying attention, you can become the best version of yourself. We all are aware of our capabilities and potential, but it is also essential that we should enhance those capabilities and become the best version of ourselves. Winfrey advises, "A true sign of confidence is when you can break away from the crowd, regardless of what others say or think."

❑

Books and Oprah

Oprah's relationship with books has been that of a friend. Often when she was in need of guidance and companionship during her childhood, found comfort among books. She likes to read the works of the famous writer Maya Angelou. It was her biography, *'I Know Why the Caged Bird Sings'*, that left a deep impression on her and helped her emerge out of the turbulent phase of depression in her life. Later in her life, she went on to make good friends with Angelou.

There are number of books that Oprah has co-authored and authored. She also had many books written on her. The list of those books goes as follows:

- *In The Kitchen with Rosie: Oprah's Favorite Recipes* (1994) with Rosie Daley
- *A Journal of Daily Renewal: The Companion to Make the Connection* (1996) with Bob Greene
- *The Uncommon Wisdom of Oprah Winfrey: A Portrait in Her Own Words* (1997) with Bill Adler
- *Journey to Beloved* (1998) with Ken Regan
- *Make the Connection: Ten Steps to a Better Body and a Better Life* (1999) again with Bob Greene
- *Oprah Winfrey Speaks*
- In the episodes of 'The Oprah Winfrey Show', she has many times recommended several books to her audience. These books go a long way in enriching her audience intellectually. The list of her recommended books goes as follows:
- *'The Four Agreements: A Practical Guide to Personal Freedom'* by Don Miguel Ruiz (This book by Don Miguel Ruiz, simple yet so powerful has made a tremendous difference in how I think and act in every encounter – Oprah)
- *'A Return to Love'* by Marianne Williamson (This book made me realize that there are only two emotions, love and fear. In every relationship you are moving toward one or the other – Oprah)
- *'To Kill a Mockingbird'* by Harper Lee (Harper Lee's masterpiece, my favorite novel of all time, traces one

lawyer's effort to defend a wrongly accused black man without sacrificing the innocence of his children – Oprah)

- *'Their Eyes Were Watching God'* by Zora Neale Hurtson (Zora Neale Hurtson's classic is my favorite story of all times. Janie Mae Crawford spends almost two decades with abusive dominating men but eventually finds true love with tea cake. In the time they are together, he teaches her to open her heart to the world – Oprah)
- *'Power of Now'* by Echkart Tolle

Oprah's Book Club

Oprah's Book Club was a book discussion club segment of her talk show. It highlighted books chosen by Oprah. She started the club in 1996, with the selection of a new book, generally a novel, for her viewers to read and discuss every month. It ended its decade-long run along with the show, i.e., on 25 May 2011. During its run, it recommended 70 books over the course of 15 years.

Due to its widespread popularity, several vague and unknown books managed to become extremely popular, augmenting their sales by several million copies. Al Greco, a Fordham University marketing professor, estimated the total sales of the 69 'Oprah editions' at over 55 million copies.

The book club has witnessed many literary controversies, for example, Jonathan Franzen's public dissatisfaction with his novel *'The Corrections'* that was chosen by Oprah, and the infamous case of James Frey's memoir, A Million Little Pieces, a 2005 selection. The controversy led to Frey and publisher Nan Talese confrontation.

On Friday, 1 June 2012, Oprah announced the launch of Oprah's Book Club 2.0 with Wild by Cheryl Strayed. The new version of Oprah's Book Club, a joint project between OWN: The Oprah Winfrey Network and O: The Oprah Winfrey Magazine, will incorporate the use of various social media platforms and e-readers.

In April 2000, Oprah and Hearst Magazines announced 'O', The Oprah Magazine. It is a monthly magazine, and in no time, it has become today's leading women's lifestyle publication. It is the most successful magazine launch in recent history and presently boasts of a circulation of more than 2.35 million readers every month. In April 2002, Oprah went on to launch the first international edition of O, The Oprah Magazine, in South Africa. The magazine extends her 'live your best life' message to another audience of the continent.

❑

Quotes by Oprah Winfrey

1. A gift isn't a gift unless it has meaning. Just giving things to people, especially children, create the expectation of more things.
2. A world of possibilities awaits you. Keep turning the page.
3. After all these years, I could say thank you to a woman who had a powerful impact on my early life.
4. All life is energy and we are transmitting it at every moment. We are all little beaming little signals like radio frequencies, and the world is responding in kind.

5. All stress comes from resisting what is.
6. All you need to do is know who you are.
7. Alone time is when I distance myself from the voices of the world so I can hear my own.
8. Always listen to your inner voice.
9. Be quiet. Part of your responsibility is to honour the quiet inside yourself so you can hear the call.
10. Breathe. Let go. And remind yourself that this very moment is the only one you know you have for sure.
11. Connect. Embrace. Liberate. Love somebody. Just one person. And then spread that to two. And as many as you can. You'll see the difference it makes.
12. Dare to be different. Be a pioneer. Be a leader. Be the kind of woman who in the face of adversity will continue to embrace life and walk fearlessly toward the challenge.
13. Death shows up to remind us to live more fully.
14. Do not waste your time with people who have shown you they mean no good for you.
15. Don't complain about what you don't have. Use what you've got. To be less than your best is a sin.
16. Don't waste your time in the race looking back to see what the other guy is doing. It's not about the other guy. It's about what can you do. You just need to

run that race as hard as you can. You need to give it everything you've got, all the time, for yourself.

17. Don't worry about being successful. Worry about being significant.

18. Education is the key to unlocking the world, a passport to freedom.

19. Even in bad times, always say thank you. Whatever you are going through, God is using you to get through. God has already put a rainbow in the cloud.

20. Every one of us gets through the tough times because somebody is there, standing in the gap to close it for us.

21. Find the courage to seek out your big dream, regardless of what anyone else says or thinks.

22. Follow your feelings. If it feels right, move forward. If it doesn't feel right, don't do it.

23. Follow your passion. Do what you love, and the money will follow. Most people don't believe it, but it's true.

24. Forgiveness is letting go of the hope that the past can be changed

25. God can dream a better dream for you than you can!

26. God can dream a bigger dream for you than you can dream for yourself, and your role on Earth is to

attach yourself to that divine force and let yourself be released to it.

27. Good luck—it's always ready to use in the case.
28. Gratitude is the single greatest treasure I will take with me from this experience.
29. Great communication begins with connection.
30. Happiness is there for the taking—and the making.
31. I believe everyday your life speaks to you—through every experience, through the people you meet, and even though pain, fear and self-doubt.
32. I can't imagine I could have become the person I am now without books. Books became synonymous with freedom. They showed that you could open doors and walkthrough.
33. I do not believe in failure. It is not a failure if you enjoyed the process.
34. I feel that luck is preparation meeting opportunity.
35. I have a lot of things to prove to myself. One is that I can live my life fearlessly.
36. I truly understand that there is a lesson in everything that happens to us. So I tried not to spend my time asking "Why did this happen to me?" but trying to figure out why I had chosen this.
37. It is very true, that the way you think creates reality for yourself.

38. Joy is a sustained sense of well-being and internal peace—a connection to what matters.

39. Joy is one part of inner peace, one part giddy delight and 100% attainable.

40. Know this for sure: When you get the chance, go for it.

41. Let passion drive your profession.

42. Life is better when you share it.

43. Live life and take chances. Believe that everything happens for a reason and don't regret. Love to the fullest and you will find true happiness in life. Realize that things go wrong and people change, but things do go on. Sometimes things weren't meant to be. What is supposed to happen will work its way out?

44. Love is a lesson worth learning.

45. Luck happens when preparation meets opportunity.

46. Making a different choice allows you to live a different life.

47. Material success is rewarding and a lot of fun, but it's not the most important thing in my life because I know when this is all over, the Master isn't going to ask me how many things I owned or how many television shows I did. I think the questions will be what did I do to make a difference? Did I learn to live with love in my heart?

48. I would dream that she would think that's funny. There is a part of me that loves her and I watch her show every day.

49. My goal is always, how do you get better?

50. My highest achievement: never shutting my heart down. Even in my darkest moments - through sexual abuse, a pregnancy at 14 lies and betrayals – I remained faithful, hopeful and open to seeing the best in people, regardless of whether they were showing me their worst. I stayed open to believing that no matter how hard the climb, there is always a way to let in a sliver of light to illuminate the path forward.

51. My idea of heaven is a great big baked potato and someone to share it with.

52. Never for a moment allow your greatness to interfere with your goodness.

53. Never give up your power to another person.

54. No matter how diligent or persistent you have been, there is not one of us who made this journey toward success by ourselves.

55. One of the biggest mistakes humans make is to believe there is only one way. Many diverse paths are leading to what you call God.

56. One of the things that I encourage for anybody interested in their charity or philanthropy is to start from where you are and what has mattered to you.

57. People make things happen. All the rest is just window dressing

58. The purpose is the thread that connects the dots to everything you do that leads you to an extraordinary life.

59. Remove the fear, and the answer comes into focus.

60. Skiing is the next best thing to having wings.

61. Sometimes you find out what you are supposed to be doing by doing the things you are not supposed to do.

62. Spirituality for me is recognizing that I am connected to the energy of all creation, that I am a part of it and it is always a part of me.

63. Surround yourself with only people who are going to lift you higher.

64. Take the ideas that speak to you. Use your imagination. Create something wonderful.

65. The best way to look at ageing is to see it as an opportunity to leave what didn't work behind and step boldly into a brand new future.

66. The biggest adventure you can take is to live the life of your dreams.

67. The biggest mistake in helping undeserved kids is not raising the bar high enough. Children will believe if you believe in them.

68. The future is full of possibility, whether you make one tiny change - or a whole invigorating, thrilling, inspiring bunch of them.

69. The greatest discovery of all time is that a person can change his future by merely changing his attitude.

70. The happiness you feel is in direct proportion to the love you give.

71. The ultimate comfort zone is within.

72. Understand that the right to choose your path is a sacred privilege. Use it. Dwell in possibility.

73. Unless you choose to do great things with it, it makes no difference how much you are rewarded, or how much power you have.

74. Until we rise in the streets and change the laws in this country, this will continue to happen and every time it will be more heinous than the next.

75. Walkthrough life eager and open to self-improvement and that which is going to best help you evolve, because that's really why we're here: to evolve as human beings.

76. We are each responsible for our life-no another person can be.

77. We can't become what we need to be by remaining what we are.

78. We're all here to figure out how to best give ourselves away.

79. What I find powerful is a person with the confidence to be herself.

80. What I know for sure is that pleasure is energy reciprocated. What you put out comes back. Your base level of pleasure is determined by how you view your whole life.

81. When I didn't have friends, I had books.

82. When I learn something when I know something when I find something. I always want to share it. Because life is better when you share it.

83. When women put their heads together, powerful things can happen!

84. When you do your best, people notice.

85. When you give up on life, never give up on yourself, because there is so much for you to keep on giving!

86. When you learn, teach. When you get, give. Maya Angelou taught me that.

87. When you live with an open heart, unexpected, joyful things happen.

88. Where there is no struggle, there is no strength.

89. You are built not to shrink down to less but to blossom into more.

90. You are not your circumstances. You are your possibilities. If you know that, you can do anything.

91. You are responsible for your life. It doesn't matter what your Mama did. It doesn't matter what your Daddy didn't do. You are responsible for your life.

92. You are the single biggest influence in your life.

93. You are where you are in life because of what you believe is possible for yourself.

94. You become excellent, and when you become excellent, no-one can take that away from you.

95. You don't become what you want, you become what you believe.

96. You have two choices: You can come down from the mountain and spend the rest of your days thinking it was so beautiful there, or you can create a vision, look upward, see the next mountain, and start the climb all over again.

97. You must feed your mind with reading material, thoughts, and ideas that open you to new possibilities.

98. Your greatest power is to show love, to receive love and to be love.

99. Your intention rules your life and determines the outcome.

100. Your work speaks for you. Your art defines you.

❑

Timeline

1954: Oprah Gail Winfrey, the illegitimate child of Vernita Lee and Vernon Winfrey, was born on January 29 in Kosciusko, Mississippi, where she lived until the age of six with grandparents Hattie Mae and Earless Lee.

1960: Oprah went to live with her mother, Vernita, and half-sister, Patricia, in Milwaukee, Wisconsin.

1962: Oprah spent a brief time with her father, Vernon, and stepmother, Velma, in Nashville, Tennessee, and attended East Wharton Elementary School in Nashville.

1963: While living with her mother in Milwaukee, Oprah was raped by a cousin and victimized by other sexual predators.

1968: Oprah received a scholarship to attend Nicolet High School in Milwaukee. Vernita sent Oprah back to Nashville, where she gave birth to a son who died shortly afterwards. She attended East Nashville High School, from which she graduated in 1971. While there, she was a member of the drama club, the National Forensics League, the honor society and the student council, and was voted the most popular girl of the senior class. She also served as a representative to a White House Conference.

1969: Sometime this year, Oprah began to keep a journal, which she still maintains.

1970: While representing Nashville station WVOL, Oprah won the contest for Miss Fire Prevention. She also was selected as the first Miss Black Tennessee.

1971: Oprah graduated from high school and won a scholarship to Tennessee State University. She was hired to read the weekend news at radio station WVOL and on occasion read the weekday news.

1973: After working for a time at station WLAC, Oprah went to its television station, WLAC-TV. She left college before graduating to accept a job in Baltimore.

1976: At station WJZ-TV in Baltimore, she worked as a reporter and co-anchor of an evening news programme. There she met production assistant Gayle King who became and remains her closest friend.

1978: At WJZ-TV, Oprah was taken off the evening programme and made co-host of the morning show People Are Talking.

1984: Oprah accepted a job in Chicago as host of A.M. Chicago.

1985: Oprah met Stedman Graham, who was to become her 'significant other'. She also met Quincy Jones, who offered her the role of Sophia in *The Color Purple*, for which she became an Oscar nominee.

1986: Her programme was renamed The Oprah Winfrey Show. It had been purchased by the King Brothers Corporation and was nationally syndicated. Oprah also appeared in the movie Native Son, a film based on the Richard Wright novel. She purchased her

Chicago penthouse condominium on the lakefront. Oprah was a guest at the marriage of her friend Maria Shriver to Arnold Schwarzenegger in Hyannis, Massachusetts.

1987: More than a decade after leaving Tennessee State University, Oprah was granted a degree in speech and drama and delivered the commencement address.

1988: Named Broadcaster of the Year by the International Television and Radio Society, Oprah was the youngest person to receive the award. She began to produce her show after gaining ownership and control of it. Naming her production company Harpo, she purchased the studio facilities, becoming the first black woman to own a studio and production company. She bought a farm in Indiana. In later years, she purchased two other homes, one in Colorado and one in California. Her friend and assistant, Billy Rizzo, died of AIDS, the disease that was to kill her half-brother.

1989: Jeffrey Lee died of AIDS. With another investor, Oprah opened a restaurant, The Eccentric.

1990: Oprah produced the television series The Women of Brewster Place, which was dropped after 10 weeks.

She also produced and appeared in the film Listen Up: The Lives of Quincy Jones.

1992: Oprah made the documentary Scared Silent. She met Bob Greene, who became her fitness trainer and friend.

1993: Oprah appeared in the television film There Are No Children Here, which she also produced. President Clinton signed the National Child Protection Act that Oprah had initiated.

1995: Knopf published In the Kitchen with Rosie, a cookbook written by Oprah's chef with some input from Oprah. Bob Greene's book Make the Connection was published under the names of Bob Greene and Oprah Winfrey. Oprah ran in and finished the 25-mile Marine Corps Marathon.

1996: Oprah was given the George Peabody Individual Achievement Award. She produced Waiting to Exhale. Texas cattlemen brought a suit against Oprah for disparaging beef. Oprah met Dr. Phil McGraw in Texas, where he became one of her advisers. The book club became part of the television show.

1997: Oprah created the 'Angel Network'. Oprah appeared in and produced the television film Before Women Had Wings. Oprah gave the commencement address at Wellesley College, from which Stedman Graham's daughter was graduating. Art Smith became Oprah's chef and wrote a cookbook.

1998: Oprah Winfrey Presents produced the television miniseries The Wedding starring Halle Berry. Dr. McGraw joined Oprah's television show. Oprah received a Lifetime Achievement Daytime Emmy Award. Oprah starred in and produced the movie Beloved. She was described in Time as one of the twentieth-century's 'most influential people'.

1999: CBS Corporation bought the King Production Company. Oprah bought a share of the Oxygen Cable Network. Oprah's company presented the television film Tuesdays with Morrie.

2000: O magazine was launched; the international edition of the magazine was published a few months later. Oprah won the beef defamation suit.

2002: Harpo Productions developed a programme for Dr. McGraw. Oprah was awarded an honorary doctorate from Princeton University. Oprah received the Bob Hope Humanitarian Award. Oprah and Stedman stayed at the home of Nelson Mandela in South Africa. The book club was discontinued.

2003: Oprah received the Marion Anderson Award. Oprah joined with a number of world-famous people to celebrate Mandela's eighty-fifth birthday. Oprah's half-sister, Patricia Lee Lloyd, died of a drug overdose. The book club was reborn. Oprah became the first black American billionaire.

2004: The 2004 Nobel Peace Prize Concert was hosted by Oprah and Tom Cruise. Named by TIME as one of the 100 people who most influenced the 20th century.

2005: *The Color Purple* was made into a Broadway musical of which she was a producer. She became the first black woman listed by Business Week as one of America's top 50 most generous philanthropists.

2006: On 9th February, she signed a 3-year contract with XM Satellite Radio to establish a new radio channel based in Chicago. Starred in the movie Charlotte's Web playing Gussy.

2008: The Discovery Health channel was turned into OWN: Oprah Winfrey Network. The channel was delayed.

2011: Winfrey celebrated the launch of her TV network, dedicated to entertainment and lifestyle programming.

2013: Donating $12 million to the National Museum of African American History and Culture, Oprah was awarded the Presidential Medal of Freedom by President Barack Obama.

❑